Dr. Mattie Moss Clark

Climbing Up The Mountain

The Life and Times of a Musical Legend

Eugene B. McCoy

SPARROW

Sparrow Press
Nashville, Tennessee

Published 1994 in Nashville, Tennessee, by Sparrow Press, and distributed in Canada by Christian Marketing Canada, Ltd.

Printed in the United States of America

98 97 96 95 94   5 4 3 2 1

Library of Congress Cataloging-in-Publication Data

McCoy, Eugene B.
        Climbing up the mountain : the life and times of a musical legend   / Eugene B. McCoy.
            p.   cm
        ISBN 0-917143-32-9
        1. Clark, Mattie Moss.   2. Gospel musicians—United States—Biography.
        I. Title.
        ML420.C535M35   1994
        782.25 ' 4 ' 092—dc20
        [B]   94-35097
                                     CIP
                                     MN

All Scripture is from the King James Version of the Bible.

Cover design by Glynn Chisholm
Book design by Mike Goodson

Contents

Preface 1

1 Set Apart for God 5

2 Finding the Way 17

3 Giving God Everything 29

4 Yes, Lord 45

5 Here Comes God 57

6 Be Still and Know That I Am God 65

7 Master Teacher 73

8 A Legacy of Changed Lives 81

Appendices 89

Preface

After having worked closely with Mattie Moss Clark for more than thirty years, I am so pleased to have the opportunity in writing this book to show the genius of her musicianship and the phenomenal anointing of God on her ministry and life.

Mattie and I met while I was the choral music teacher at the Willow Run High School in Michigan. I saw her train—in a matter of minutes—a group of singers to sing material unfamiliar to them. I was amazed enough by that feat to place a call to her one Monday morning in 1960. That call led to a regular Monday morning call for the next three years.

As we talked, Mattie and I would extol the name of God and talk of his goodness. The presence of the Holy Spirit was evident even through the phone lines. Afterwards, Mattie would go to her basement and compose those soul-rending compositions now well known by gospel music lovers. We became servants in Christ together, as well as associates and friends.

When she was appointed president of the National Music Department of the Church of God in Christ, she called me with the good news. And I rejoiced with her, because her longing to serve was finally fulfilled. After proving her consecration, discipline and musical genius, she could function in her God-given place of authority as teacher and mentor for singers and musicians all across the country.

Mattie appointed me dean of the National Music Department and we have worked together in the Lord for many years since and continue to this day. After years of fellowship, I came to know what she wanted to accomplish almost as second nature. I knew, because I knew what she was about—she had been gifted with an anointing that could not be denied.

I asked her one day why she thought the

Holy Ghost had bound us together in his service.
She exclaimed, "Elder McCoy, I was anointed. You
were anointed. The Lord put our anointing
together to put it on others."

And this he did.

1

Set Apart for God

$\mathcal{A}$ small Catholic college in Detroit was the unlikely setting for a gospel music workshop and a concert scheduled later in the evening. At the workshop, the leader, a woman of great intensity and conviction, began instructing the nuns about the Holy Ghost, especially how he comes and works in our lives. The nuns were visibly moved by the teaching. With tears rolling down their cheeks, they asked question after question, gaining renewed knowledge of the Holy Ghost.

As the time approached that evening for the concert, there was an air of excited anticipation on the campus. After having experienced the moving of the Holy Ghost during the workshop, the nuns were eager to experience the same again. They were thirsty for more, yet unsure what to expect. This music was so different from the Gregorian Chants to which they were accustomed.

As the concert began, the Michigan State Choir, conducted by the charismatic workshop leader, was introduced and began singing gospel songs. Their dynamic leader led them from one song to the next, until a driving momentum took over. And with the singing of the last song, the anointing of God broke forth. The power of God was so strong the Catholic sisters began shouting and jumping with joy. Caught up in the anointing they tearfully found a spiritual freedom they had never known before.

The dynamic director used by God to minister on that campus was Dr. Mattie Moss Clark, best-selling Gospel recording artist, internationally esteemed music teacher and choral director and president of the music department of the Church of God in Christ (COGIC).

The impact she had on this Catholic campus in her short time there was not unique. In a long

and productive life for God, she introduced the
Holy Ghost to thousands of people, leading them
to experience the same anointing that fell that day
on the Catholic sisters. One of the greatest gospel
artists of all time, Mattie Moss Clark was
recognized in 1981 for her outstanding
contributions by Trinity College, who conferred
upon her the degree of Doctor of Humanities.

From her earliest days, God's hand prepared
Mattie for the momentous task ahead. Born in
Selma, Alabama in 1925, she was the second child
of Fred and Mattie Moss. The family eventually
grew to include six boys and two girls. A religious
family, the Mosses were poor, but they were close
and happy and surrounded by love.

Mattie's mother was a strong influence on
her—musically as well as spiritually. A pianist and
guitarist herself, she insisted that Mattie take piano
lessons. Little Mattie started playing the piano
when she was four, and at age five she was playing
for her mother's church services. Initially licensed in

*Mattie and her daughters
in the early years*

the ministry in the Methodist church, her mother had left the denomination to seek deeper depths in the Lord. Mother Moss started the House of Prayer Movement, continued singing gospel and became a strict adherent of Pentecostalism. Mattie played for her mother's mission services and traveled with her.

Mattie's siblings also were musical. Three of her brothers played instruments and all enjoyed singing. Her brother Edwin, who eventually became a music teacher, trained her to play the piano and helped develop her apparent musical skills. Her mother always encouraged Mattie in her music. More than once, she told her daughter of seeing a vision of Mattie leading a choir that could not be numbered. Unfortunately, her mother never lived to see this prophecy realized.

Mattie's school activities revolved around music, and she often could be found playing the piano for the choir and for other musical groups in the school. She also sang and came to love it as well.

Turning Points

After completing high school in Selma, Mattie dreamed of attending Fisk University in Nashville, Tennessee to study classical music and choral singing. She wanted to have a choral group sing with a symphony orchestra, something that had never been done before.

But circumstances intervened. Her father died, and Mattie remained home with her mother and attended Selma University instead. According to Dr. Clark, this was one of the turning points in her life orchestrated by God. Instead of following the path of becoming a classically trained musician, she continued traveling with her mother, providing music for the church services.

In 1947, Mattie joined her sister in Detroit, a move that would change her entire direction and become yet another turning point in God's plan for her life. In the small town of Selma, Mattie felt the security of belonging to a family that was well known and well respected.

But Detroit was another story altogether. In the big, cold, anonymous city, Mattie felt alone. Her insecurities drove her to search and reach for new depths in God. Her musical gifts gave her a sense of identity and a place to belong, as she started playing piano for churches.

In Detroit Mattie met and married Elder Elbert Clark, a Church of God in Christ pastor. God blessed their union with children, all close in age. During this time, Mattie's reputation as a musician and church leader began to grow. She directed Cadillac Motors' Christmas choir for eleven years and also conducted mass community-wide choirs for the prestigious NAACP Freedom Fund Dinners. Mattie believed with all her heart that the Lord would do something for her and that she would do something for him.

In the beginning she felt that her five daughters (Jacky, Denise, Elbernita or "Twinkie", Dorinda and Karen) and one son (Leo, the oldest of her children) might hinder her ministry. However, she was determined not to slow down, so she simply gave her children back to God, and in the process, she trained and prepared her daughters for ministering in music.

Passing It On

Mattie wasted no time teaching the girls to sing. At age two, her youngest, Karen, was standing on the offering table at Bailey Temple in Detroit singing for the congregation.

Sometimes the Lord gave Mattie a song in the early hours of the morning. Rather than wait for the dawn, she would wake the children and in spite of much crying and complaining about having to get out of bed at that hour, she would teach them the song. What she heard from the Lord she gave to the girls, encouraging them and nurturing their budding musical talents. And under their mother's tutelage, they progressed rapidly.

"I remember playing in the streets," Karen recalls, "and our mother would call us in to work on a song. I thought it was unfair at the time, but now I see it helped us to grow together as a family." As they grew up, Mattie formed the girls in a group and called them The Clark Sisters. As the girls entered their teens, it became clear to them and their mother that their future was in professional Gospel music.

After appearing on a number of their mother's records, The Clark Sisters made their album debut with *Jesus Has a Lot to Give* in 1973. A string of releases followed, including *The Clark Sisters, Is My Living in Vain, You Brought the Sunshine, Bringing It Back Home Live* and *Heart & Soul,* a Grammy Award nominee in 1987. The Clark Sisters have appeared in films, on television programs, and in theatrical stage plays. They've toured the nation and the world, delivering high-energy concerts.

But behind the scenes, their mother's spiritual and musical influence is evident. As Jacky says, "People need to realize that what we do isn't just singing and speaking. It's also in the living. Our whole purpose is living a life devoted to the Lord."

Known for her vigor, enthusiasm, intensity, precision and drive, both in her life and her concerts, Dr. Clark made a strong impact on her daughters. "Even now, many people who see us refer to us as Mattie's daughters. So it's like she's always there. She wanted us to sing and be a part of everything she was doing," recalls Jacky. As Mattie recalls, she taught them "to leave everything behind when their feet hit the platform, and give God their all."

And that distinctive of The Clark Sisters also is the hallmark of Mattie Moss Clark's life.

Mattie's daughers

Jacky

Denise

Dorinda

Karen

"Twinkie"

l-r, top: Jacky, Karen,
Mattie, Twinkie
bottom: Denise, Dorinda

The Clark Sisters today

2

Finding the Way

$\mathcal{D}$r. Clark's first choir position in Michigan was
with Detroit's Greater Love Tabernacle Church of
God in Christ, pastored by the late Bishop William
Rimson. She trained his choir for three years. After
serving as staff musician for the Blessed Martin
Spiritual Church, Mt. Moria Women's Chorus and
the McFall Funeral Home, she became the
musician and choir trainer for Bailey Temple
Church of God in Christ where she spent thirty-
five years with the late Bishop John Seth Bailey.
Bishop Bailey was presiding bishop of the
Southwestern Michigan Diocese of COGIC and
Dr. Clark became the state president of the music
department. This meant she was to prepare
appropriate music for the State Ministers and
Worker's Meeting as well as for the State

Convocation. It was here in the Southwestern Michigan Diocese that the gospel music of Mattie Moss Clark would have its genesis and eventually escalate to heights that only the Lord could know.

The state music department was made up of district choirs that sang when their respective district made a presentation during the state meeting. The choirs, based on the number of churches in the district, ranged in size from exceptionally small to very large.

Dr. Clark felt the system in place was an ineffective way to get singers together for the state convention. She prevailed upon Bishop Bailey to allow her to create a state choir made up of singers from throughout the various districts. Thus, the famous Southwest Michigan State Choir was born. Dr. Clark's idea of having a state choir for state conventions caught on and eventually spread throughout COGIC.

Soon, COGIC members began to view state meetings with much anticipation because the state choir would be singing. What they saw was not only a choir distinctive because hundreds of singers sang together, but a choir that was trained by Dr. Clark to sing with the power of the Holy Spirit.

The anointing was the foundation of Dr. Clark's life and ministry. It is that manifestation of the Holy Ghost that imparts ongoing power to effectively accomplish whatever the Lord has said to do. Scripture tells of the anointing of David:

Then Samuel took the horn of oil, and anointed him in the midst of his brethren: and the Spirit of the Lord came upon David from that day forward . . .

(1 Sam. 16:13)

Until this time, choirs usually stomped, screamed and made much noise as a substitute for the anointing. But Dr. Clark had a different idea for this choir. The motivation and the emotion needed to come from within, from the Holy Ghost.

It was no easy task to introduce this new concept to the choir, but Dr. Clark was more than up to it. God had prepared her for this assignment, and she took it on enthusiastically. The choir members gladly accepted the teaching of their determined leader. And once they experienced the anointing she taught about, there was a difference in their presentation, a power not seen before.

Dr. Clark never wearied at the task of working with the choirs, but continued energetically knowing this was an integral part of the ministry God had given her. She was not only to demonstrate the anointing by her life. She also was to make certain that as many people in her choirs as possible began singing and playing with the anointing. She was confident that when that happened, yokes would be broken and people would find the freedom of the Lord—because all things were being done to the glory and honor of God.

Making Her Mark

As Mattie Moss Clark fulfilled her mission from God, she left her mark on COGIC. After her appointment as national president of the music department in 1968, she intensified her efforts to work with musicians and choir members across the country instilling in them a responsibility to Christ as well as a capability for Christ. Young people in particular received her, and many were saved, inspired, refreshed and uplifted by her music, message and method.

As she has done with any task she has taken on, Dr. Clark revolutionized the COGIC music department, leaving a rich and colorful legacy in her wake. She gave definition to the role of State Minister of Music, implementing structural and organizational changes in the music department. Her state church had recognized her by giving her the authority to follow her calling and this was impacting her music ministry.

In her travels, she taught singers her songs.

Planning session for the
State Convocation

The Michigan State Community
Choir, with their leader
Dr. Mattie Moss Clark

When it was time for the national convocation, she rallied choir members for the national choir. She had laid the groundwork by teaching a few of the songs prior to the singers attending the convocation. As a result of her traveling, her first choir rehearsal was merely to perfect songs she had already taught.

After two years of working with the national choir, Dr. Clark received a call from Presiding Bishop J. O. Patterson. The Bishop informed her that he saw a need for a music convention to train singers and musicians, and asked her to organize and convene the convention. She considered his invitation a privilege, and thus was born the National Music Convention of the COGIC. COGIC always has been richly blessed with musically talented young people. Dr. Clark recognized that raw talent and through the National Music Convention challenged those young people to sharpen their talents and give them back to God so he could use them. And, she challenged them to pass on to other singers and musicians what they learned so that others also may excel in the music ministry.

Awesome Movements of God

Dr. Clark convened the first National Music Convention in Detroit, followed by conventions in Atlanta and New Orleans. The objectives of the conventions were to:

1) Train musicians and singers for effective service in their church and in their communities.

2) Present concentrated class offerings for the COGIC musician and those with limited musical knowledge in order to meet the first objective.

3) Show choir success by combining music and the anointing.

Each convention did see an awesome demonstration of God's presence. God used both prayer sessions and workshop sessions to manifest his power. The first thing every morning, singers and musicians could be seen literally running to prayer service. During the general assembly, young people experienced salvation through Jesus Christ and the baptism of the Holy Ghost with the Word of God going out in power.

A favorite part of the convention was "A Song Is Born" night, an event created by Dr. Clark to showcase new talent. This inspiring night of music often was the driving force behind the outstanding recordings made at the conventions.

The National Music Convention attracted both accomplished musicians and people with no knowledge of music. No matter their level of music familiarity, they came for powerful teaching in the day sessions by national dean Eugene B. McCoy and powerful singing at night, led by Dr. Clark.

Finding Power in the Music

Dr. Clark directed Eugene McCoy to formulate workshops that served a number of functions. First, these workshops were to sharpen the musical skills of singers and musicians. Second, they were to instruct musicians in choir etiquette. And, third, they were to encourage attendees to adopt a mindset of ongoing music ministry. Those who attended the workshops heard emphasized over and over that their music was to be a ministry, and that both choir members and musicians alike must be saved and baptized with the Holy Ghost for effective music ministry.

Often, first-time choir members and musicians came to the workshops unaware that there was power to be released by singing and playing instruments. But Dr. Clark and McCoy taught and demonstrated this principle untiringly and effectively, and no one left without seeing firsthand the difference between "performance as usual" and anointed music.

Three God-given Tasks

With the advent of the COGIC National Music Convention, Dr. Clark finally could accomplish on a grand scale what she felt God had given her to do. And she felt God had given her three main tasks.

First, she was to demonstrate the anointing in all of her life, not just in spiritual things. When the Lord called Dr. Clark to this work, the Spirit of the Lord came upon her from that day forward. Not only singers and musicians benefited from her dedication to ministry. She has taken into her home people from the streets who needed a place to stay. And, she has believed in, stood by and encouraged many people when others would have nothing to do with them.

Second, she was called by God to gather young people—to sing, but also to experience the baptism and the anointing of the Holy Ghost. Without the anointing, young singers tended to rely on fleshly emotions to carry their songs, often leading to an attitude of glorifying the flesh. She constantly witnessed to young people without Christ, and many were saved. Every choir rehearsal Dr. Clark held throughout the country became a platform for her to proclaim to those who were lost that "Salvation Is Free."

Third, Dr. Clark was to show the world that the supernatural functioning of the anointing erases the impossible and causes the possible to be seen clearly, especially in difficult situations, so that the name of God is glorified. Her life became a testimony to that supernatural power.

3

Giving God Everything

In order to have creative impact, composers must possess a certain individualism. They must dare go against the conventional, bringing fresh new ideas to the music. Originality and an innate flair for musicianship also play an important role.

Mattie Moss Clark's impact as a composer dramatically changed gospel music throughout America. Under her influence, singers became artists and pianists and organists became musicians. They were propelled to fantastic musical heights in gospel music.

What set apart Mattie Moss Clark and her style of gospel music? What uniqueness was there about her that influenced so many in gospel music? She felt that God is worthy of praise and that men

A television appearance with the
Michigan State Community Choir

With the Michigan State
Community Choir

and women must dedicate themselves to him with a dedication that lasts for life.

Always a perfectionist, Mattie would not settle for being average, but instead glorified God with everything in her. For her, the aim was not merely to succeed but to exceed. She fasted and prayed in order that she would belong totally to the Lord. That kind of sacrifice of self made it possible for her to receive an astonishing anointing of the Holy Ghost that pervaded her entire life.

I Can Do Nothing

She captivated audiences, musicians and singers by creating in them a hunger and thirst for the anointing. Creating this hunger in others for the Holy Ghost became a hallmark of her life. She experienced what it was like "to do all things through Christ that strengthens me" (Phil. 4:13). Others might talk about the power of God and its application to one's soul, but Dr. Clark made it clear that the anointing is to be demonstrated—not talked about.

As we saw in the previous chapter, David was anointed king, and from that time the anointing was with him. Likewise, when the anointing fell on Dr. Clark it did not leave. This is evident by watching her and hearing her, and by the influence she has on so many.

She says it more eloquently, "Without the anointing, I can do absolutely nothing. It is the power of God that has pervaded me. As I yield myself to him and am obedient, the anointing blesses everyone around."

When seemingly unsolvable problems confronted her, there was a power moving in her to bring victory. With every victory, God placed a song in her spirit that related to the problem. All she had to do was listen to the song God gave, and the solution to the problem became evident. This miraculous working of God caused others to glorify him and strengthened their faith.

Bringing Them In

Because Dr. Clark's music, in the Jubilistic Pentecostal style, strongly appealed to those outside COGIC it gave the denomination a new prominence. Persons from many other denominations began to attend COGIC churches to hear this new sound that emanated from a people they once considered lower in status than those in other denominations.

The people who made up the beginning of the movement were predominately from a rural and poor background, often without much formal schooling. Many of the more formally educated people would not identify themselves with these saints, because they considered them to be ignorant and unlearned.

Because those outside the movement did not understand the working of the Holy Ghost, they were shocked at how God blessed the ministry of these people. They could not explain how this movement developed and grew. The biggest shock

came when members and even leaders of other
denominations began to leave their churches to join
the holiness group. Once they came, many of these
outsiders sat under Dr. Clark's tutelage and
attended rehearsals and sang with the choir.
After having heard the anointed music of Dr. Clark,
pastors of churches in other denominations began
having her music played in their services. They even
insisted that only certain ones could perform her
music—"the born-again ones."

Today Mattie says that if she had the
opportunity to start over, she would include persons
from every denomination in her choir, training and
developing them alongside her COGIC choir
members. Why? "Because the anointing brings us
together," she said. "And once you get the real
experience, you can't let go."

In the holiness church, congregational singing
was a big part of the total worship experience.
COGIC churches, particularly, have a legacy of
spirited, upbeat, happy singing in their services. In

any congregation could be found people saved, sanctified and baptized with the Holy Ghost. Therefore the congregational singing had strong appeal because the anointing from the Holy Ghost was dominant in the singing.

Mattie took the Jubilistic Pentecostal sound of congregational singing with its steady driving percussion beat and tailored it to choral music. But it concerned her that the emphasis often was more on the beat than on the music and the lyrics. She felt it time for the anointing to be introduced to the performances so that they would be more effective in ministering to those who heard.

Putting Life in the Music

Dr. Clark came on the gospel music scene at a time when, as she describes it, "[choral] music was flat and there was no life in it." Part of the "flatness" of the music, she felt, was that not everyone who sang gospel had been born again. Inherent in gospel music is a deep emotion that can lead singers, if not

saved, to take on an assumed piety. The Bible says
they have a "form of godliness, but deny the power"
(2 Tim. 3:5). Then onto the scene burst Dr. Clark
with this bold statement: "I know what they need,"
she said. "They need the anointing." What was
missing from the music, she felt, was the
manifestation of God's power from the Holy Ghost.

In Five Minutes!

Elder James Whitehead, Sr. invited Dr. Clark
to his annual state music convention in Detroit at
the late Bishop P. L. Lockett's church. He
announced to the public that Dr. Clark would
prepare a choir to sing during the convention, and
that she would do it in five minutes.

Normally, it took two or three rehearsals to
prepare a choir to sing a new song. Yet this woman
was going to have a choir ready to sing in five
minutes? This was unheard of, impossible. Some
thought it simply a gimmick to entice people to
attend the convention. And the announcement did
create a stir of excitement.

Building the anointing

Mattie speaking to young people

After Dr. Clark was introduced to the vast
crowd, she asked singers in the audience to come to
the choir stand. She placed them into each of three
sections—soprano, alto and tenor. She had no bass
section, because in her compositions all the men
sang on the tenor line. Once she organized the
group, she found she had seventy-five singers.
The congregation listened intently as Dr. Clark
gave brief instructions to the choir. She taught the
singers her song, "Look and Live." After she gave
each section their part, she then had all the sections
sing together. As they began to sing, a sound
emanated from those voices that was new, spirited
and anointed.

As she directed the choir, Dr. Clark gave
them instructions. She became a different person as
the anointing flowed and as the singers followed her
in singing to the glory and honor of God. The
audience also began to praise God, not because of
the inherently emotional music, but because the
Holy Ghost was present. The anointing came upon

Jacky, Dorinda, and Mattie
raise the roof

her that night and everything was done by that anointing. And it took a mere five minutes to accomplish.

There was a full concord of sound emanating from those voices, a sound not heard before. Everyone there was astonished. As the glory of God filled the sanctuary, corporate praise and worship began to flow and the people stood, saying "thank you, Jesus" and "yes, Lord."

When those gathered began to shout "hallelujah" giving the highest praise, spiritual pandemonium broke forth.

A New Sound

The incredible musical experience that night forever changed the face of gospel music in Detroit, particularly in the Church of God in Christ, and subsequently throughout the country.

Others wanted their church choirs to recreate the new sound they heard. But they discovered the only way that joyful, heart-stirring sound could be recaptured was by the anointing.

The brief rehearsal that was part of the service that night became a trademark of Dr. Clark's choir rehearsals. Usually choir rehearsals began with a song and the Lord's prayer. Often the chaplain in the choir led devotions. Then the choir practiced a song in preparation for Sunday morning worship. As one might expect, Dr. Clark's rehearsals were different. Before she began to rehearse the choir, she held a singing, prayer and testimony service, where she exhorted the choir members to "sing until the Lord comes in."

And he did come in. During the services prior to rehearsal, many singers and musicians were saved and baptized with the Holy Ghost. Those singers then became easier to reach musically and spiritually because God had touched their spirits. The atmosphere set prior to rehearsal transformed what happened later as the singers began singing to the glory and honor of God.

Musical Changes

Dr. Clark added her own touches to the music. Besides dispensing with four-part harmony in favor of three-part harmony, she reinvented the structure of the song. Instead of the regular verse, chorus, verse, she placed a special chorus at the end that musically transformed the entire song, ending with the momentum and the rhythm at its highest peak. These touches added a bit of Dr. Clark's personality, but the anointing made all the difference.

The continuing appeal of Mattie's music was that it was rhythmic, with an accented beat. Compositions that were less rhythmic could be played on traditional pipe organs. But Mattie's music had to be played on a Hammond Organ, and required drums and tambourine too.

Churches began to bring in these new instruments so they could perform Mattie's music. The pipe organ, created for traditional hymns and classics, was left behind in the revolution of gospel music with a Pentecostal sound. The instrument simply could not duplicate the strong accented rhythmic beats of this new music.

Mass Choir, Bailey Cathedral

Mattie leads worship as only she can

4

Yes, Lord

When Mattie Moss Clark first started making appearances with the state choir, she and the choir often found themselves placed last on the program. By that time, much of the audience had left—including choirs that already had sung. By the time Dr. Clark and her choir sang, there was only a sparse crowd left to hear them.

Rather than getting discouraged, Mattie continued on with her task of introducing the Holy Spirit to others. "I wanted the opportunity to bring about God's anointing," she said, and it didn't matter whether it was to a few or many. Her choir may have been the last to sing, yet the power of God through their anointed singing electrified the audience that was left. Those who heard the choir reacted similarly to the Samaritan woman at the

well with Jesus—they left and told all that had
happened. The word spread and before long more
and more people were staying until the end of the
program to hear this amazing choir.

As they came to be known for the life and
excitement that they added to the musical program,
eventually Mattie and the choir were moved to the
beginning, in a place of honor.

Psalms, Hymns and Spiritual Songs

Mattie found inspiration for her music from
Scripture. "In order to be effective," she said, "I
took instructions from Ephesians 5:19 which says,
'speak to one another in psalms, hymns and
spiritual songs...' I always did my music in that
sequence."

"When composing, the Lord would give me
the name of the album then the songs to build
around that title," Mattie said. For instance, her
first album, *Lord Do Something For Me*, consisted of
the following songs:

"Lord Do Something For Me"

"Yes Lord Praise"

"Small Be Mine"

"Going to Heaven to Meet the King"

"Jesus Knows the Trouble I've Seen"

"Trust In God"

"Couldn't Hear 'em Pray"

"I Know a Great Savior"

Coming from the Spirit

Mattie's spirit was full of music and song. She listened to that music in her spirit, and then tried to replicate it. She knew exactly what she wanted and would not accept anything less than what she heard.

Sometimes that determination to replicate only what she heard in her spirit was misunderstood. For instance, she was criticized for overlooking outstanding artists who could have demonstrated a song in her rehearsals, using her daughters instead.

Dr. Clark responded to that criticism. "I trained my girls to get the sound I wanted," she emphasized. "If I could not get it from others or knew that they did not have what I was after, I used the girls to get the sound."

More than any selection of singers, though, she realized that she had to depend on the anointing to replicate that sound in her spirit. "Without the anointing, I am nothing and can do nothing," she repeated. "You get whatever you desire in music with the anointing."

Her compositions evidenced a supernatural moving of the Holy Ghost. "Early in the morning I would pray," Mattie said. "Then I would fast as I did my composing. The Spirit of God gave me freedom with the authority of the Holy Ghost. As I directed, I received new ideas from the Holy Ghost. And as he has his way with me, the singers, musicians and the congregation are blessed."

Mattie's daughter Dorinda says, "Every time she leads a choir, the anointing is thrown over her.

Leading the choir at the COGIC
National Convocation in Memphis

Mattie prepares her
grandchildren to take the stage

It is so powerful, so strong." She depended on the anointing. She leaned on the anointing. The impossible always became possible. And she did not stop until she got what she wanted musically.

Making Recording History

In 1959, the first COGIC state choir was organized as the Southwest Michigan State Choir under Mattie Moss Clark. In that same year she and the choir made their first recording, *Lord Do Something For Me* on Kapp Records.

In 1963, Mattie began recording on Savoy Records where she and the choir became one of the first gospel groups to record a live worship service. Her three records on Savoy were *Wonderful, None but the Pure in Heart* and *Salvation Is Free.* One song, the Church of God in Christ Chant, appeared on all of Dr. Clark's albums. When the saints sang that chant, bodies were healed, souls were saved and inspiration came. It is amazing how singing the words *yes* and *yes, Lord* could cause the

anointing to fill a room with supernatural power.
Mattie wrote two hundred songs and recorded fifty
albums. According to Nash E. Shaffer, Jr. who hosts
the Sunday morning Golden Gospel radio program
on WJPC in Chicago, these Mattie Moss Clark
songs are considered musical masterpieces:

> "None But the Pure in Heart"
> "Salvation Is Free"
> "A Closer Walk With Thee"
> "Lord Renew My Spirit"
> "Write My Name Above"

Mattie's first nine albums were recorded with
the Southwest Michigan State Choir, and included:

> *Lord Do Something For Me*
> *Wonderful, Wonderful*
> *None But the Pure in Heart*
> *Salvation Is Free*
> *City Called Heaven*
> *A Closer Walk With Thee*

Show Me the Way

Lord Renew My Spirit

I'll Take Jesus For Mine

The next two albums were by the Clesiastic Sounds—*Try Jesus, He Satisfies* and *Seek Him and He Will Let. Wonderful Grace* was recorded by the Southwest Community Choir.

The Michigan State Community Choir recorded the next nine albums:

That's Christ

I Don't Know What

The Hands of God

The Wages of Sin

He Was Hung Up

I Am Crucified With Christ

Make Me That Building

I'm Not Alone

Best of The S. W. Michigan State Choir

Subsequent albums were recorded at the United National Auxiliaries Convention of COGIC ("UNAC 5"). On two of the albums, *Make Me That Building* and *I'm Not Alone,* the solos were by Mattie Moss Clark.

She said she wanted her music to be powerful enough to "hit dry bones" and shake them to the core. That she has done in her remarkable recording career.

Her songs have made an impact on the music industry as well. Many of her songs have been recorded by leading artists in the gospel field, including:

"Salvation is Free"

—Clay Evanst & Fellowship Baptist Church

—Donald Vails

"He Abides"

—Chas Taylor Singers

"Climbing Up the Mountain"

—Soul Children, New Orleans, LA

—BC&M Mass Choir

"Sanctify Me Holy"

—Chas Hayes & Church of Prayer Choir

"You Need Him Now"

—Chas Hayes & Cosmopolitan

"Beatitudes"

—Atlanta Chorale Ensemble

A Champion of New Artists

Mattie championed new artists, giving them the opportunity to appear in her choirs and introducing them through the "Back Home Hour" musicals held each night during the National Conventions. A number of those artists went on to national renown. A few of the artists she helped launch include Rance Allen, Vanessa Bell-Armstrong, The Hawkins Family, Andraé Crouch, Bobby Glenn, Beverly Glenn, Vernard Johnson, Donald Vails, Patrick Henderson, Richard "Mr. Clean" White, Benny Cummings and Keith

Pringle. Dr. Clark also introduced to record labels such notable gospel singers as Ester Smith, Betty Nelson, Douglas Miller, Kenneth Ward and of course The Clark Sisters.

She continues to train young talent as founder and president of Clark Conservatory of Music in Detroit.

Pioneering GMWA

Mattie Moss Clark also was the creative force behind Gospel Music Workshop of America (GMWA). In 1969, she and Mrs. Elma Hendricks of Detroit put together a "Sing-A-Rama" to convene at the New Bethel Baptist Church where Rev. C. L. Franklin was pastor. They recruited a 1,000-voice choir and invited James Cleveland to be the special guest. Cleveland was so taken with the idea that he set up the Music Workshop of America. Dr. Clark suggested that he add "Gospel" to the title to differentiate it from other musical groups. Thus was born Gospel Music Workshop of America, which now comprises approximately fifty chapters.

***Dr. Clark and National Dean
Eugene B. McCoy***

5

Here Comes God

$\mathcal{T}$hose who attended Dr. Clark's choir rehearsals
—whether as a singer, musician or onlooker—
found them to be unforgettable experiences. They
were really more revival services than rehearsals,
with the exhortation of God's Word and praise
preceding the learning of songs. From beginning to
end, Dr. Clark taught the singers and musicians
how to sing with God's power.

In Mattie's rehearsals, she demanded three
things from the singers: "open your mouth," "pat
your feet," and "clap your hands." These things
were so integral to a song, she felt, that it was
mandatory to do them if notes were sung. With
those verbal commands, she led the choir to
experience the chief characteristics of Pentecostal

congregational singing. When these seemingly insignificant elements were added, the music touched souls and led singers to give high praise and thanksgiving to God.

Her rehearsals were nondenominational, carried out without referencing race, creed or religious conviction. The top priority, aside from learning the music, was to let God's anointing fall. As the rehearsal began, Dr. Clark taught not only the song, but its ministry. The effect of this was to usher in the Holy Spirit, which helped them learn the music quicker.

Dr. Clark coined the phrase *the building of the anointing* to explain her method of inviting the Holy Ghost to take hold. She would assign four persons to speak, one right after the other. This she felt built the anointing to the point that during and after the last person spoke, they saw the breaking down of all walls that hindered a "going forth in the Lord" by those who were bound.

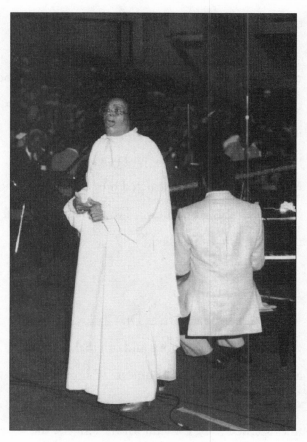

Getting the most out of her choir

That this happened time and time again in rehearsals was evidence that God was there among them.

But Mattie instructed her singers to remember that others besides themselves were to be blessed. For example, at one concert the anointing had so filled the entire building that a musician jumped off the organ seat and began to dance. Mattie immediately instructed him to return to the organ with this admonition, "You can't shout until the entire song is finished."

Nothing But the Best

Many of the phrases Dr. Clark used during rehearsals were humorous and original, but she always was able to communicate whatever she was after. For instance, when the sound was not right or lines seemed to be difficult for the singers, she would stop, exasperated, place her hand on her hips and say, "Touch somebody and tell them to quit playing hard to get. Now touch somebody else and tell them to stop playing hooky."

On other occasions, she threw shoes, purses or hymn books at the slackers in the choir, causing some to consider trying out as a catcher for the major leagues. She was a strict disciplinarian, but inattentive choir members knew there was no malice in her actions. After much laughter at her antics, the difficult line was quickly learned. She simply would accept nothing less than the best from her choirs.

On many occasions during rehearsal the sound system would go off. Quickly, Dr. Clark would tell the singers, "We are rehearsing anyway. We can't let God down because of other things happening against the rehearsal."

When difficulties arose, she would exclaim, "When the negative things arise against the singing, always know, here comes God."

The rehearsals were nearly always concert-performance quality. Dr. Clark insisted the singers give their all in rehearsal to learning the song, and this they did.

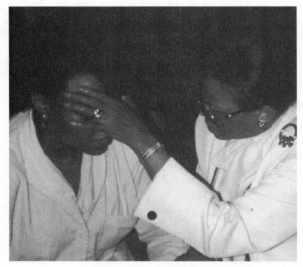

Praying for others

Rehearsals drew people not a part of the choir. If they were not saved when they came, they usually were before the evening ended. In Dr. Clark's rehearsals those who attended not only learned how to sing as a choir member, but saw a demonstration that God's way always supersedes any other way.

You Must Be Born Again

Often, songwriters who were not born again tried to capture in their music the excitement and power of Dr. Clark's music. Unsaved writers brought to gospel music their creative talent. They wrote beautiful words and music. But using these words did not bring the same result as Mattie's music did.

It could not sound the same or come in the same form. It did not yield the same results. Because the anointing only comes on those who are saved.

In Amos 5:23, the Lord said to Israel, "Take

away from me the noise of your songs, for I will not hear the melody of your stringed instruments." This verse applies to those singers and musicians who are not born again and yet write songs about God. They desire to affect the people the same way that Dr. Clark did in her rehearsals, not realizing that they "have a form of godliness, but denying the power thereof . . ."

Mattie Moss Clark always demonstrated the injunction of the Apostle Paul to "be filled with the Spirit."

6

Be Still and Know That I am God

*M*attie Moss Clark came to be known not only as an anointed artist but as a leader who could draw hundreds of young people to sing in her choirs. For COGIC members, her name was synonymous with exciting music. Wherever she was to minister there was anticipation of a spirit-filled service. People knew that with Mattie involved the service would not be a "dead" service, but one where the Holy Spirit would saturate the entire place.

Her reputation kept her constantly demonstrating the anointing. Her musicals were standing-room only. She consistently gave herself totally to God, and the more she ministered in music, the greater her anointing. As a result, Dr. Clark rose from obscurity to a giant in the music field, becoming a musical legend in her own time. Her breaking forth musically, however, was not without hindrance or pressure. As a woman working with men, she often encountered colleagues who felt she had stepped into territory reserved for the "brethren." Because her demonstration of the anointing through her music often dumbfounded many of her fellow ministers, she often was misunderstood.

Her God-given task of training choirs and demonstrating the anointing was monumental. With little support from others, she often had to defend herself and her position, standing up to whoever hindered what she knew she had to do. This gained her both supporters and detractors. With a great call on her life, Dr. Clark hoped for cooperation from pastors. She needed their backing if she was to maintain a strong national choir numbering in the thousands. She felt a choir this size was necessary in view of the millions of people associated with COGIC.

But without the pastors' cooperation that dream would be difficult to realize. At times young people were not given consent by their pastors to attend Mattie's choir rehearsals. So she would leave the choir stand in the national meeting, walk the aisles requesting that those who sing in their local choirs become a part of the national choir.

There also were logistical problems. Where would she place a choir of that size? And there were constant difficulties with the public address systems. As in most human gatherings, personality problems surfaced time and time again. Yet, despite the sometimes overwhelming difficulties, the officials of both the state and national church continued to look to her for suitable music for those special services. And she delivered.

As Dr. Clark said, "The greater the suffering, the greater the anointing and the quicker it comes when you hit the floor." All she wanted, she said, was to be allowed to "do my job."

At times, she keenly felt a lack of official backing and support. "Sometimes I felt like I wasn't needed. It was like standing in a lonely place all these years without the authority behind me," she said. "The anointing was the only thing that made me feel I belonged. I had a job to do and that kept me pushing."

There were a few supporters. Bishop J. S. Bailey allowed her to function as his minister of music without interference from other departments. "He gave me a free hand to do anything I wanted to maximize the music department in the state," Mattie said.

But that kind of support was rare. As Mattie said, "Preachers would tell me I have too much anointing, that I was too big. Finally, I asked God why I was having so many problems with ministers regarding the music ministry. This line came to me, 'Be Still and Know That I Am God.'"

"All the little trials I had caused me to write the song, 'My Soul Loves Jesus,'" Mattie said.

I won't let go his hand
I've had my share of troubles
In the midst of it all
I won't let go of his hand.

According to Mattie, "The young people and others who sat under my ministry who were not saved always asked the question, What must I do to be saved? As I looked for an answer to give to them, I wrote this song, 'Salvation Is Free.'"

Love brings salvation
Prayer brings salvation
True conservation is free
I'm glad that salvation is free
I'm glad I know that it's free
I put my trust in thee
For you to receive
For you to believe
Deliverance in the blood
From God's Holy Word

And give me peace
That salvation is free

God is my salvation
And I'm glad that it's free
He's all, and whatever you need
Have you yet trusted and believed
What God gave it's well done
All came through salvation
I know that it's free

Salvation
For deliverance in the blood
It comes from the heart
He died on the cross
I'm glad that I know it's free
I'm glad he gave it to me.

This song was so powerful that every time
Mattie sang it souls were saved.

Ministry did not come without its hardships

for this woman of God. But she kept on climbing up that mountain that God had called her to, even when things got tough. How did she do it? Once again, Dr. Clark credits the anointing of the Holy Ghost on her life. "The anointing is like a screen," she said. "So when the pressure comes, I can stand it."

The vivacious Dr. Clark

7

Master Teacher

$\mathcal{D}$r. Clark emphasized the development of each of her choir members. She believed there are four distinct areas of growth in a singer's life that need attention:

1) Intellectual. This could be accomplished through classes, class discussions, lectures, demonstrations and printed literature.

2) Spiritual. Here, she used devotions, inspirational services and ministry of the Word to allow musicians opportunities to grow spiritually.

3) Social. Because she felt it important to build unity, Mattie encouraged social activities such as fellowship services and banquets, to encourage interaction between musicians.

4) Musical. Singers had opportunity to perform individually and with groups, to learn

techniques of musicianship, to develop skill
building and to participate in individualized
lessons.

Often while training her choir members
Mattie would ask a simple question and then
enlarge upon it. From the Official Handbook of the
National Music Department (COGIC), here is her
profound answer to the deceptively simple
question, "What is a choir member?":

*A choir member is that indispensable part of the
choir which, if there were none, a choir would not
exist.*

*The average choir member does not know
exactly how important he or she is. When they do, they
become aware of the tremendous responsibility which
accompanies this importance.*

*When one feels needed, responsibility turns into
a commitment. Commitment is born out of a deep
sense of responsibility. I feel responsible as a choir
member knowing no one can take my place.*

Now, remember, you are not functioning from a selfish, egotistic posture, but from knowledge that every voice is needed. And if I do not keep my commitment, then I will not be lending the necessary support for success of the entire group.

I must always remember that as small as a flute is, that flute is needed in the orchestra. One might suppose that small flute is so insignificant that the conductor would not miss it.

However, when the conductor steps to the podium and raises the baton bringing in the first choral strain of music, he stops the orchestra immediately and asks the flute player to please begin with the full orchestra. He had not heard the flute. If the flute had not been important, he would not have stopped on the downbeat.

Every choir member should fulfill their commitment, and that is to be a good choir member. Demonstrate a strong sense of belonging. Be secure in your spot. Do not allow through neglect your spot to become insignificant.

Laziness, indifference, selfishness, lack of motivation and a stream of other negatives can cause choir members to lose their sense of belonging.

Following instructions and directions is a necessary part of the commitment. Rebellious and stubborn choir members can cause nothing but havoc in a choir.

Those words were for the singers. But the musicians did not escape Dr. Clark's scrutiny. She had words of wisdom for them too:

Have you ever wondered what the task of the musician is in the overall musical aggregation? You say, to provide the music, of course. Well, that's partly correct. However, there is really more to it than that.

You see, a musician provides accompaniment for the singer or singers. That is, accompaniment goes along with the singer. The singer, in this instance, is to be heard distinctly and the musician who is really an able musician complements the singer and never allows his music to override nor overshadow the singer.

A good accompanist is able to help a singer or group of singers become inspired with their own singing, thus allowing for the anointing of the Lord to take over both the singer and musician. When this happens, God's name is thereby glorified. That's what it's all about.

What is it that would cause a musician to become harsh, raucous and loud with his music? There are several factors that we need to observe.
First of all, a snappy, syncopated introduction has a tendency to turn on the listening audience.
Nothing is wrong with that. You are for those few moments in the limelight. Now, cool it, for the singer is ready to sing. In other words, you decrease so that the singer can increase.

Secondly, some musicians have gone on an ego trip and have never returned. These are the ones who feel as though God meant for only them to play and no one else. The really amazing thing about it all is that these folks do not know the difference between their emotions and the anointing.

Thirdly, there are some musicians who will not hear anyone because the tendency to believe, "I have arrived to a place now where no one can tell me anything."

To avoid these insidious pitfalls, simply remember who you are spiritually, discipline yourself under the influence of the Holy Ghost, and remember to do all to the glory and honor of God. Success then is yours.

Discipline can come when it is understood by the musician that the style of playing which is done during the testimony service ought to be different when accompanying a singer. Both are art forms and certainly should not resemble each other. Just as the Negro Spiritual has a distinct mood and sound which is different from the mood and sound of Black gospel, so the disciplined musician distinguishes himself by furnishing proper mood music, if you will.

Practice, practice, practice regardless of how proficient you feel yourself to be. The more practice, the better one becomes. Don't allow yourself to become satisfied with merely getting by or anything will do.

Improve upon that which you feel you have perfected. You will be absolutely amazed to find out how much more you can perfect it. However, if you do not try it, you never will know . . . will you?

A master teacher through her words and actions, Dr. Clark inspired, challenged and encouraged her musicians and singers to become all that God intended them to be.

8

A Legacy of
Changed Lives

When a gospel music audience does not respond to the music, when the hand-clapping, foot-patting and shouting at the singers is absent, it is said that the audience is "dead."

But Dr. Clark points out that songs are never dead.

"The third verse of Psalm 33 says, 'Sing unto the Lord a new song...' and we ought to make every hymn of praise a new song," she said. "We are not to present old worn-out praise, but put life and soul and heart into every song." It's easy to do this, she says, if "we remember we have new mercies every day, and experience new beauties in the work and word of our Lord."

Again in Psalm 47:6, we are exhorted to
"Sing praises to God." According to Dr. Clark, if
we see this as a happy and glad work, we shall never
let the music pause. God never ceases to be good,
therefore we must never cease to be grateful.
"When he has all our praise," she said, "our
gladness and joy will not be expressed in groans but
in songs coming from hearts the Holy Ghost is
touching on a daily basis."

"When your feet hit the platform everything
else should be absent except that of singing to the
glory of God with the rich anointing beginning to
saturate you," says Dr. Clark.

Singers saturated with the oil of gladness
make a joyful noise unto the Lord, causing men
and women, boys and girls, to lift their hands and
sing to the glorious name of our sovereign Lord.
Will any sound do when "making a joyful noise?"
Based on Psalm 47:7, Dr. Clark responds with a
resounding "NO": "... sing ye praises with
understanding," the Scripture says. The

understanding is enlightened by the Holy Spirit, she points out, causing us to be fully capable of offering worthy praise.

Singers were exhorted by Dr. Clark to understand what they were singing. Sing and think; think and sing, she would say. She led her singers to follow the summons, "For the Lord is a great God and a great king . . . above all gods." From those scriptural exhortations to praise God, singers would begin to thank and praise the Lord and even dance before him, prior to, during and after the rehearsal.

These experiences impacted the lives of many singers and musicians from across the country and the world as well. The impact felt or seen was the same regardless of denomination, race, creed or color. The anointing, manifesting itself from the Holy Ghost, always was awesome. It gave people freedom in their spirits to be what the Lord wanted them to be, for "where the spirit of the Lord is, there is liberty."

Dr. Clark's daughter, Elbernita, better known as "Twinkie," says that she would watch in awe as her mother, powered by the anointing, began to effect change in singers' lives. "She is a woman with tremendous wisdom from God," said Twinkie. "She always worked with us, showing us how to manifest the anointing."

On occasion when teaching a song, Dr. Clark would not hear the instrumentation the way she wanted it. She would instruct Twinkie to play it her way. Twinkie would protest, telling her mother it would not work that way. But Dr. Clark told her to try it anyway.

When Twinkie played the music as her mother asked, she found that it did work— wonderfully well. Incidents like these convinced Twinkie that her mother was an anointed master teacher. Trained by her mother, Twinkie went on to become one of the renowned gospel musicians in America.

To Dr. Clark, the music was to be part of an

ongoing glorification of God. Her daughter Dorinda, who not only sings but also ministers the Word of God, said, "When I first started speaking I was afraid and really didn't know what to do. My mother told me not to be afraid and simply lean on the anointing, that the Lord would teach me there on the spot. Just as my mother said, the Lord filled my mouth as I began to speak and freedom welled up in me as the anointing took over."

She continued, "I have never seen another person like my mother who applied the anointing in every facet of her life and was always successful and effective."

Because of the eternal focus of her ministry, the impact Dr. Clark has had on gospel music will never cease. Because of her total yielding to the Holy Ghost, she was given the task of demonstrating to others the power of the anointing. And she has been faithful throughout her life. Dr. Mattie Moss Clark truly is God's anointed one.

Dr. Mattie Moss Clark,
God's anointed one

*Editor's note: On September 22, 1994, as this book
neared completion, Mattie Moss Clark went home to
be with her Lord.*

PRAYER

Father, this is the day which you have made and I shall rejoice and be glad in it. My soul magnifies you. My spirit rejoice. My, how good you are to me. My mind is getting better. It is being quickened to righteousness.

My whole aim is to please you.

Strengthen those who are soldiering for you and cause them to fight the good fight of faith. Allow their will and determination to be enmeshed into you causing them to experience your anointing upon them. And in so doing every yoke will be destroyed to the glory of God with the work of God going strong.

I love you because you first loved me and gave yourself as a ransom that I might have the right to the tree of life.

I need help and that right quickly. Touch me again with your finger of love causing a special anointing to come over me and deliver me from myself. I thank you and praise you for grace. Bless all those around me with your sweet benediction and your special favors as they work in the Lord's vineyard. My soul says 'Yes'!! AMEN.

Appendix A

An Overview of Gospel Music

The traditional Black spiritual, as we know it, was born during the days of slavery. What set the text apart was a religious theme dealing with "freedom afterwhile"—not in this life but in the life to come. The Black spiritual is based on the idea that the Savior would eventually "avenge his elect" and there would no longer be turmoil, sadness or despair, but rather a life of joy, peace and happiness.

The slaves sang songs of hope such as "Didn't My Lord Deliver Daniel, Then Why Not Every Man?" Their foremost desire was to make heaven their home. "City Called Heaven," "Live-a Humble" and "Lord I Want to Be a Christian" evidenced this desire to go home to heaven. Inherent in the Black spiritual is a beauty and finesse of sound rooted in the religious fervor, humbleness and simplicity of an enslaved and oppressed people. These slaves sought after God so wholeheartedly that they were given a musical style to leave as a legacy to the world.

Lest we tend to glamorize the experience of slavery, it should be noted that this lack of freedom affected them mind, body and soul. Their longing for freedom is evident in the following lyrics of "Freedom Afterwhile":

Freedom afterwhile
Freedom afterwhile when I get home

These songs were not songs of joy, but rather of faith and hope. The joy would come later, after their sorrow and suffering had ended. Their unswerving faith, even though enslaved, was so strong that one stands in amazement. Their religious fervor was carried over into the Black spiritual, giving it its warmth and stirring emotion. The lyrics of the Black spiritual expressed the depths of human suffering, along with a hope of ultimate deliverance. All the hardships, oppression and unwarranted suffering of the Black servile status are poignantly expressed in the spiritual. Their sorrow was so deep, but their ultimate destiny was heaven. This strong and determined hope is expressed in the lyric of "I Got a Robe":

I got a robe
You got a robe
All of God's children got a robe
When I get to heaven
Gonna put on my robe
I'm going to walk all over God's heaven.

With the Emancipation Proclamation, slaves were given their freedom, and Christian folk everywhere rejoiced. A revival broke out and people sang songs full of religious ecstasy, excitement and joy over this gift the Lord had granted to them. No longer did the lyrics of songs deal with the desire of the slaves for freedom from their oppression and hardship. Rather than "Freedom Afterwhile," the lyrics now reflected that new freedom experienced here and now, as in "Free At Last":

> I'm free, I'm free
> I'm free good Lord
> Thank God Almighty
> I'm free at last.

This new form of music became known as new spiritual or gospel music. The word *gospel* refers to "good news," and the good news of these songs was "I'm free at last!"

Gospel music expresses religious freedom. Freedom and all that it brought to the former slaves created in them a new song. This joyous, happy, exciting song gave thanks to God for deliverance. Because of their deliverance, the people felt that God should be praised and served hereafter. Gospel music is full of deliverance and hope, with the ultimate hope of entering into heaven. The songs "Someday, Somewhere, I'll Make It Somehow" and "If You See My Savior" are evidence of the hope that is still a theme of the religious Black community.

Gospel music plays an important part in churches, often dominating the service. The highlight of the service is the music selection prior to the minister's sermon, a piece that prepares the people for the sermon to come.

Gospel's rhythms and harmonies are a combination of the old spirituals and the syncopated sounds of today. These songs are strong on encouragement to Christians. The experience of being converted is recalled by a Thomas Dorsey song "I Can't Forget It, Can You?"

Even another comes to mind ("I'll Never Forget"):

Jesus, I'll never forget
What you've done for me

Jesus, I'll never forget

How you set me free

Jesus, I'll never forget

How you brought me out

Jesus, I'll never forget

No ....never.

There are songs that express the Christian's joy: "I'm so Glad Jesus Lifted Me," "It's in My Heart" and "Happy in the Service of the Lord." The lyrics of another Dorsey song, "Singing in My Soul," depict that great joy known by children of God:

I'm singing in my soul

while the billows roll

I sing from morn 'til night

It makes my burden light

I'm singing in my soul.

Even the titles of these songs express "good news."

Gospel songs do not limit their focus to the present only, but also to the future and after death. The hope of people in past and present generations for heaven is shown in "When the Gates Swing Open," "Inside the Beautiful Gate," and "I'm on my Way to Heaven to Meet the King."

Some gospel music titles are on the lighter side. One gospel writer entitled a song "Life is a Ball Game," then related each base to some aspect of life. Another song is entitled "God Don't Need No Matches, He's Fire by Himself."

Religion was a tremendous force in the Black community not only during the days of slavery, but also today. Gospel music still dominates and exerts a strong appeal because of its theme of ultimate deliverance from human suffering.

I know the Lord

Will make a way

Yes He will

Although you may not

Have a friend

He'll go with you until the end

I know the Lord

Will make a way

Yes He will.

Others have used this chorus:

Have you tried Jesus?

He's alright

Have you tried Jesus?

He's alright

Yes I've tried him, Yes I've tried him

He's alright

Yes I've tried him, Yes I've tried him

He's alright.

The gospel music that still brings hope today has its roots in the church with its prime purpose being to activate and enliven the worship service.

But Black music was not placed in its proper perspective until it began to be written down by men such as H. T. Burleigh, William Dawson and others. Since that time, Black music, particularly the spiritual, has found has found a respectable position in the standard and classical repertoire as pure folk music.

Gospel music has not yet reached the musical heights of respectability of its counterpart the spiritual. Even though gospel is a direct outgrowth of the spiritual, it did not inherit musical respect. As the spiritual did, gospel must make its own way.

The haunting and plaintive melodies of the spiritual linger long after the music ends. Likewise, the gospel song's syncopated rhythms and melodies linger long after one has heard them. The magnetism of gospel is this: It draws the ear of the listener, creates excitement that engulfs everyone in its grip and compellingly breaks down inhibitions. The result is a sea of feet patting, heads moving, hands clapping and bodies swaying as the whole congregation lifts spirits of praise to the Lord.

The Recordings of
Mattie Moss Clark

(oldest to newest)

1. Lord Do Something for Me

2. Wonderful, Wonderful

3. None but the Pure in Heart

4. Salvation is Free

5. City Call Heaven

6. A Closer Walk With Thee

7. Show Me the Way

8. Lord, Renew My Spirit

9. I'll Take Jesus For Mine

10. Try Jesus, He Satisfies

11. Seek Him and He will Let

12. Wonderful Grace

13. That's Christ

14. I Don't Know What

15. The Hands of God

16. The Wages of Sin

17. He was Hung Up

18. I am Crucified with Christ

19. Make me that Building

20. I'm Not Alone

21. Best of the Southwest Michigan State Choir

22. "UNAC 5"

The Clark Sisters Discography

1994	Miracle	Sparrow
1990	Bringing It Back Home, Live	Rejoice/Word
1988	Conqueror	Rejoice/Word
1986	Heart and Soul	Rejoice/Word
1984	Sincerely	New Birth Records
1982	You Brought the Sunshine	Sound of Gospel
1980	Is My Living In Vain	Tomato
1979	He Gave Me Nothing to Lose, But All to Gain	Sound of Gospel
1978	New Dimensions of Christmas Carols	Sound of Gospel
1978	Count It All Joy	Sound of Gospel
1976	Unworthy	Sound of Gospel
1974	The Clark Sisters	Bilmo
1973	Jesus Has a Lot to Give	Bilmo

Words of Praise for Dr. Mattie Moss Clark

BEBE WINANS
Sparrow/Capitol Recording Artist

"I love Mattie Moss Clark because she is a pioneer. She taught me how to be a pioneer, to be determined. By being those things, you can accomplish anything. She proved it with her life. Thank you for your life, Mattie."

CECE WINANS
Sparrow/Capitol Recording Artist

"Mattie Moss Clark is a great teacher. She trained people to do their best—nothing less than the best. You can see that through her daughters."

NASH E. SHAFFER, JR.
WJPC Radio, Chicago

"I first became familiar with Dr. Mattie Moss Clark at the age of nine, when my church choir performed her compositions. I've been in gospel radio for 11 years, and I love to play the legendary songs of Dr. Clark, including "Climbing Up the Mountain" "Write My Name Above" and "None But the Pure In Heart."

"Dr. Clark brought the COGIC to its height of spirituality and placed it on the musical map. She birthed music that has been untouchable throughout the years. Her impact spread to the other denominations as well, causing many to start replacing their pipe organs with a Hammond B3, drums, guitars and tambourines. She trained me and many others in the art of preparing a new choir on a song in 5 minutes.

"Mattie built a strong foundation in the COGIC denomination by instructing a generation of young people who serve today as its leaders. She believes in a consecrated, spiritual lifestyle, which commands genuine respect in all who have studied under her or know her. She is a pacesetter, a pioneer, and a tremendous woman of God."

MADAME MATTIE WHIGLEY
Vice President, National Music Department, COGIC

"Mattie and I have served faithfully together for 25 years. We met in 1968 and I became her Vice President in 1969, working together to this day. We recently honored her at a banquet in Detroit, celebrating her silver anniversary (25 years) with the music department of COGIC.

"Mattie is the greatest musician I have ever known. She is a talented pianist, organist, singer, director, speaker and teacher. She does it all! She is a licensed missionary for the denomination, and has helped many, many young people and adults to learn about music and discover God's anointing. She fasts and prays, and receives her music and direction straight from the throne of God."

AL HOBBS
President, Gospel Music Workshop of America

"When many in the music business were busy becoming legends in their own minds, Mattie

Moss Clark became a legend in her own time. Gospel Music and the world are a better place because of Dr. Mattie Moss Clark."

FRED HAMMOND
Commissioned

"Dr. Mattie Moss Clark was one of the few people who helped Commissioned in the beginning of our career. She gave us our first big break in Memphis, Tennessee. Helping us with that crucial first step, in a real sense, was responsible for the widespread acceptance of Commissioned today."

RICHARD SMALLWOOD
Recording Artist

"I began listening to Dr. Clark's music when I was a teenager. Songs like 'Climbing up the Mountain,' 'Never Turn Back' and 'Salvation is Free.' These songs inspired me to begin to write my own original compositions. Dr. Clark has been such an encouragement to me in my music ministry, always saying, 'Son, be encouraged. I love your music.' Coming from such a pioneer and a legend in gospel music, her encouragement has meant the world to me. Dr. Clark, I love you!!"

REV. LAWRENCE ROBERTS
Pastor, First Baptist Church, Nutley, NJ
(Former Savoy Records Producer)

"Mattie is a remarkable songwriter, director, singer and musician."

TERESA HAIRSTON
Publisher, Score Magazine

"Mattie Moss Clark is the premier female choir director. She pioneered the demonstrative style of teaching and directing that inspired generations of gospel artists."

VANESSA BELL-ARMSTRONG
Recording Artist

"Mattie Moss Clark, to me, was the godmother of Gospel music. She was the only mother that I knew. I thought of her as a mother, because she took me under her wing when I was 13 and gave me a chance. She taught me, every time I opened my mouth, to sing like it is my last time. She is brave and loyal. She is strong, steadfast, and determined. She is the blessed one, a most anointed writer and singer. God gave to her, so she gives back to God. That's what she means to me. She's just music. She's lovely, and I love her."

RANCE ALLEN
Gospel singer, pastor and preacher

What comes to mind when I hear the name of Dr. Mattie Moss Clark is the memory of being a young boy, and looking up to this very pretty, elegant lady. She was beautiful, but had the presence of a giant. She was at the top of her craft, and has been so influential in my life.

Mattie opened a lot of doors for me in the area of choir music, in the Church of God in Christ. She introduced me to the UNAC church, giving me an opportunity to preach that lead to my participation in the National Convention. She was a lady who didn't believe in doing anything half way. If you're going to do anything, do it with all your might or leave it alone! Because of that I have been able to do so many things myself. She was such a great example to learn from. She practiced what she preached. I remember being at her house one day and she telling me that I was going to be a great musician and signer. I was just a little boy then, but she just kept on stressing that if I stayed with the Lord and did what he said, there was no limit to what I could do and where I'd go. She was a strong believer in putting God first. She is a lady I am proud to know. I appreciate all she has done for me and many, many others.

DOLLY KELLY

"It is because of you that I am who I am today. I love you. You always will be my best friend, my auntie."

Dr. Mattie Moss Clark
Current Recordings
Available

- *The National Church of God in Christ National Convention Choir, Live in Atlanta*

- *Dr. Mattie Moss Clark Presents: The Michigan State Mass Choir*

- *The Clark Family Live* (Available January 1995)

Check your local Christian bookstore for these and other Sparrow cassettes and compact discs.

SPARROW